# Zero Hour

# Zero Hour

Kristjana
Gunnars

Red Deer College Press

The Publishers
Red Deer College Press
56 Avenue & 32 Street Box 5005
Red Deer Alberta Canada T4N 5H5


Design by Peter Bartl/word and image
Typesetting by Boldface Technologies Inc.
Printed and bound in Canada by
Gagné Printing Ltée.


Canadian Cataloguing in Publication Data
Gunnars, Kristjana, 1948–
Zero Hour

ISBN 0-88995-066-0 (bound)
ISBN 0-88995-064-4 (pbk.)

1. Gunnars, Kristjana, 1948–   – Biography
2. Authors, Canadian (English) – Biography*
I. Title
PS8563.U574Z53 1991 C813'.54 C90-091756-3
PR9199.3.G85Z475 1991

"When the hand of the clock falls,
then time is over for me."
— Goethe's *Doctor Faustus*

For Tove, my mother

To write you this I have come to the Gateway to the West. Not because the West is intriguing. But because it is there: open, dry, with little culture and much politics. And beyond the West there is the ocean. The jungle. The rains. That is a place to long for. To think towards. I think towards the western coastline of this continent, where mist is in the air.

It seems quiet, but that is an illusion. The quiet is in the soul. Out among the elm branches, the wind blows. Cars drive on the streets. Children squeal in yards and on sidewalks. Birds chirp loudly under house gables. Mailbox lids slap in the morning search for letters all along the street. But in my soul there is a great silence.

I have come to that place in life where there is nothing below. There are no lower numbers.

I have heard of *ground zero* writing.
I imagine it is a writing in which the
author does not know what to do. There
are no assumptions to draw on. Nothing
is understood. Culture has vanished.
Writing is enacted exactly where the
bomb fell.

There is only a vague memory of something lost. A hazy recollection that this
place was once occupied. There were
tears. Laughter. A smile. A forlorn look
charged with sorrow.

It is probable that you do not know how
you feel when you know the bomb is going
to fall and explode where you are standing: when you prepare for it. You get the
medicines. You put blankets on beds.
You build ramps for wheels. And when
the explosion happens, you are running.
Helping. You turn. Help is needed and you
help. You do all this and you do not know
how you feel.

Only later, after, do you know. When it is
over. The dead are in the ground. There

has been a clean up. Then you realize
there is a feeling in your chest. You are
angry. Suddenly you scream, your mouth
open. You are surprised at the sound
you have made. You did not know this
sound was in you. It comes from the deep
caverns you have not seen, where forms
pass, shadows cross, and you do not
know what they are.

Perhaps it seems like a bomb, but that is
an illusion. There has been no bomb. Only
a loss, as if a world has gone away, and a
revelation that sometimes a world goes
away and never returns.

When a world disappears, it takes away
with it everything you are up to that
moment. Your past is erased within a few
minutes and you no longer recognize it as
your own. Suddenly you stand up and find
you have to start over. There is no you.
Your personality, culture, knowledge are
gone and there is nothing in their place.
You have become an alien. A foreigner.
You recognize none of the social customs
others take for granted. Your priorities

are different and you do not know where you got them. They are there, but they are not your own.

I have been present on two such occasions when such a bomb fell and I was changed from one person into another. At the birth of my son and the death of my father. It is like moving into a new home. The old one was familiar. You were comfortable, you had a routine, you recognized the neighborhood. The new home is an empty shell. The street is unfamiliar, the neighbors are strangers, the smells, sounds, colors are jarring. There is no furniture, no rug, no lamp. The linoleum on the floor is brown and uninviting. The grey wood has white paint spots on it. None of the door handles are on the doors.

I did not know where we were. He did not tell me and I did not ask. It was just north of Victoria on Vancouver Island, in that West which is rain forest and mist. We drove on the highway crowded by pines and alders and then into a dark and spacious park. Here were the cedars that grow for hundreds of years. We came to a river. It was not wide and not very deep, but along the banks on both sides lay hundreds of dead salmon. They had traveled all this way, to the place of their birth, only to beach themselves and lie stinking in decomposing shades of grey and mold, their mouths gaping, their eyes bulging.

I am glad certain souls are meant to travel along the same roads. It is less lonely that way. He was the writer Bill Valgardson, whose path mine has crossed a thousand times. We were hiking under the heavy shadow of enormous pine trees. *The most powerful symbol of our time*, he said, *is the mushroom cloud.*

When I came to the Gateway to the West, I had nothing with me. I arrived in Winnipeg in a very small red car with one red dress in the passenger seat. It was a dress I had never worn. Before this I had never liked the color red. But that day I was prepared to tolerate it the way I was prepared to tolerate whatever came my way. I was a different person. After the car and the dress, I had only the shirt on my back and very limited funds. Only later did I remember I had a typewriter in the trunk.

When a bomb falls in your life, you can do one of two things. You can glue yourself into your old life, place, routine, and repeat to yourself every day that only peripheral things have changed, only marginal things. You are still the same and daily life goes on and soon you will forget that worlds collided a short time ago.
Or you can allow yourself to feel as lost as you do feel. You can say to yourself: a world disappeared and took me with it. I will never be the same. I will never get over it. And you can leave it all behind. Go away with nothing and build something new.

I took the second choice.

Or rather the choice took me. It is possible we never choose for ourselves. We are instead swept along on waves of circumstance and emotion. There are very few choices to make. Not much we can do.

There was a Scandinavian Club dinner. This was in the West of my dry parched memory where all has been left open to the winds: Saskatchewan. I am not a club person who belongs to groups in order to have places to go. But I was writer in residence in Regina city and attended at their invitation so we could meet each other.

There were many tables, much pickled herring and entertainment: music, speeches, dances, and a comic. A clown. During dinner I found that my dinner companion at my table was the clown.

He was not funny. His name was Kolskog and he was from Swift Current. He spoke seriously at the table, but when he got up to perform he was funny. His children all did well. He said: I told them, *if you're uncomfortable somewhere, get the hell out*. Right away. This is why they have all done well.

I thought about that long and hard. I was still thinking about it when I drove out of town in the small red car. It must be true, I thought, and I am a fool.

In an essay called "Against Joie de Vivre" Joseph Epstein writes that he does not care for the things people do when they are pretending to have fun: dinner parties, picnics on yachts, gallery openings. He does not like "joie de vivre." This is because for a brief moment sometime in his early life he thinks he knew real joy. Since then he has been unable to settle for less.

There is something here I recognize. When a bomb falls you emerge as someone who is not in the game. You seem to realize that everyone is playing a game and you are not in it.

It is surprisingly difficult to tell how you are feeling. You know from somewhere how you should feel and you have a sense that you are inadequate because that is not how you feel at all. There is a tacit acknowledgement that human emotions are not all equally pretty.

I find there is a laundering of emotions going around. Certain human experiences are made to come out sentimental. Birth and death are sweetened.

Yet I can sense in the hollow cavity of my chest that birth and death are not sweet. They are awful. They wipe you away, everything you were up to that moment. There is a great loss and a great unknown: an uncertainty the human mind must be unable to cope with. You are disappearing. You want to scream. You know nothing will ever be the same and everything you know is unalterably lost.

The little red car had been used very seldom. Mostly it was in the garage. I was not familiar with it or else I had forgotten my former familiarity.

It was hot and dusty in Saskatchewan when I drove from Regina city to the Gateway to the West. I counted the kilometers on the odometer. Suddenly the odometer was showing an incredible distance covered in a remarkably short time. The numbers rolled around on the meter at breakneck speed. I punched it back to zero and it rolled forward again equally fast. I punched it back to zero again and again.

It may have been at Sintaluta. I stopped at a gas station and asked the attendant if he could fix an odometer gone berserk. He said: *I wouldn't want to touch it.*

I drove on. Later, perhaps at the Manitoba border, I noticed the odometer was quite accurate. I had simply been looking at it wrong. It occurred to me that somewhere between Sintaluta and Moosomin my mind had temporarily left me. Or malfunctioned. I thought of the mysterious disease that grips the people in Marquez's *One Hundred Years of Solitude*: they forget everything. Necessity requires them to pin notes on all their gadgets with instructions on how they work.

When tornadoes blast through in the West, we at the Gateway hear about it. How severe wind tunnels touch down in Prince Albert and Weyburn, roofs are blown off houses, barns collapse, mobile homes are lifted and deposited in ditches. At the Gateway we may see an evening sky turn grey, blue, and maroon, with thick cloud covering the setting sun. We may feel peripheral winds stretching tongues into our streets. There are rumors of summer hail. But for us the day continues to turn into night peacefully. We see the darkening sun rays behind the brown margins of cloud.

This is where the grain that grows in the vast fields between the Shield Country and the Rockies is gathered and stored. From here it is distributed to the East. This is also where the goods manufactured in the East are collected, sometimes assembled, and sent onto the dispersed farm hamlets and colonies, the tiny country communities with one church at the center of town. This is the city of the warehouses.

When I arrived I found a mansion. An old estate located in a park of such mansions, secluded by three enormous gates through which you pass. I met a thin lady whose name was Jo. She told me I could have one floor of her mansion. It may have been built and owned first by one of the owners of a warehouse during the heyday of the Exchange District.

I accepted. She was tying up yarn ends on a rug. The sun was beaming. She said: I have finished what I was doing here and now I want to go to Mexico. *It's the doing that excites me.*

At the breaking of dawn, five a.m. or so, it is so quiet that the screeching of birds in the trees echoes from empty street to empty street. The early air is flat, grey. Slowly sun rays appear. Streaks of yellow light crawl along the street, filtering through the crowns of high elms. The tops of the trees bathe in the sun. The cool air begins to warm. A jogger appears and runs around the corner. A grey cat looks up from the bottom of the stairs, beady-eyed.

On his deathbed, my father was very quiet. For six weeks he lay on a high bed in a small room. On one wall were shelves lined with baskets of all shapes and sizes. On another wall were shelves full of science books he was no longer able to read. Beside his bed was a small table with medicines. At the foot of his bed stood an easy chair where we could sit and let time pass in his presence. But in that room time did not pass. All times of day and night were the same for him. He lay very still and spoke less and less. By the end he said nothing at all.

That year the beauty of spring in the Willamette Valley was terrifying. Rhododendrons, azaleas, begonias, cherry trees, magnolia trees all stood in bloom along the streets. The air was charged with the perfume of blooming flowers. The blue jays and robins cried and laughed their bird calls in all the bushes and branches. The grass was deep green, the cedar stark rust. The sun shone orange into the valley. The beauty was painful.

I came into my father's room. He looked at me, intensely as always, his blue eyes effervescent. I asked him how he felt. He said: *here I am like Don Quixote, battling my private windmills.*

Just southwest of Regina city the land is not farmed or irrigated, so it is the kind of desert you find on the high prairie. The soil is caked dry and is fine and dusty if you crumble it. Now and then scrub brush sticks out and gopher holes abound. If you stare at the plateau, over its pale grey, brown, and straw colors, you will see a gopher put its head out of a hole, look around, then emerge altogether. There it will stand on its hind legs, look around again, and dash off. Or it will go down again into the hole. A tumbleweed may blow by on the breeze, circling like a cart wheel across the plain.

I often went across the plateau, breathing air so dry the sinuses felt singed. It was a frequent thought that a place could not be more empty than this and still be a place. Yet I knew it was not true. There was plenty there if one cared to analyze the minutiae of the prairie soil and plains scrub. Plenty of insects, wild plants, particles in the air. But it was a mental emptiness of a kind: as if no one had ever walked here before.

It is an unnamed place, I thought. A landscape without language. Before language.

Then one day I discovered how wrong I was. I went out across the desert on my usual route, expecting nothing. Only parched mud and dead weeds scratching up dust as they are thrown forward in the wind. Suddenly I encountered an assembly of people. One hundred, two hundred or more, gathered in the sun.

I stopped and realized they must all be Cree. Natives from around Saskatchewan must have traveled to this spot for some reason. They had four enormous drums with them. These were positioned at four corners of the assembly, in four directions. Around each drum sat several men holding drumsticks. There were men, women, and children milling about, some sitting on the ground, some standing, some covered in blankets or shawls.

In the crowd I recognized a man I knew. He was an elder from the Navaho tribe from the southern United States. I remembered him for his beautiful voice. When he spoke, the voice sounded so fine I thought the birds would stop singing. He motioned to me that I could join in the proceedings. I went in among them and sat down quietly. I was thinking I must have walked into a powwow in progress.

The Navaho elder stood before them all and explained that a certain woman, Anna, from the Cree tribe, had lost her father. She was in grief. It is a tradition that the grieving one be allowed to dance. *Let her dance away her grief*, he said.

The men around the drums began to beat them slowly and sonorously. Anna went into the circle, a large shawl draped over her shoulders which she held together with her hands. She stepped in rhythm to the drums, placing each foot on the ground twice. Quietly, without expression except for her empty eyes, she paced her way around inside the circle, making large circles of her own.

She danced like this alone for some time. Eventually people began to join her, one by one, and by the end a larger part of the assembly was dancing with her, showing solidarity with the grieving.

If time could be rolled back, I would go into that dance now. It struck me: *they were not talking.* It was pure loss. Loss without commentary.

I think it is time to stop all activity. To make a point of doing nothing. To sit in the sunroom, the huge windows open wide, and listen to the hammering rain fall down. Watch it drop from the sky in torrents, thunder grinding in the clouds, lightning flashing. All is dark and grey. Green leaves droop with the weight of rain. Birds fly furiously over-head in a great hurry, wings flapping desperately.

It is good to do nothing. To sit still and let the thoughts occur in their own time, at their own speed. To force nothing. To insist on nothing. Just to be and let living be enough.

---

I sometimes think life does not pass; it accumulates. You live in a certain way and eventually your surroundings have got you like a puppet. Your obligations, possessions, routines, the expectations of those around you have evolved. Your identity is not you: it is what is expected of you. It is your lifestyle.

It happens that your real loves slip out of your life. You did not notice. They are gone. You have forgotten what they were.

---

Jo, the thin lady who owned the mansion I found, gave me the key to the second floor. I unlocked the door and went in. There were many rooms in all directions. In each room there were many windows: high and wide, the way they built them eighty years ago, with windowsills. The windows looked out on all sides of the house. The floors were bare, the walls painted white.

All the windows were open. I went from room to room and birds were screeching in the branches at every window. The sun shone into one room, then moved to the next, and on around the house. It was empty and private. A blessedly empty and private place.

I thought: I want to put nothing in here. To let it stay empty. I want to be free.

---

There are mornings when you have no emotions. You are numb. You see the sun is pouring in through the window. You know it will be a glorious day. You make a cup of coffee. You put your sneakers on and walk to the corner bakery and buy fresh biscuits. You are in the sunroom, all windows open wide, and you listen to the world. But you are numb.

Other people have talked too much. They have not allowed the silence to expand. No sensations have unfolded. There is no understanding in the bones, only intellectual decorations. Commentary that has no meaning. You know if they do not stop talking you will be lost in their words.

And you have gone away to a place where no one can find you. As the warm sunny morning blazes at the world, you notice you are numb. It occurs to you: perhaps I did not get away in time.

My father deteriorated for four years. It was a gradual physical weakening that we all thought was temporary. His left side was not fully functional. Eventually he could not use his left leg much and had to give up running, then walking. Soon he was walking around the yard, dragging his left leg. His condition was occasioned by a benign tumor in the brain.

On occasion he collapsed with an epileptic-like seizure. When he had an extreme seizure in early March, he was sent to the hospital in Portland for further tests. When he went there, I flew in from Canada.

It was not the beginning of the end. It was the end. It was the countdown: five weeks to death. To zero.

The decline and fall of my father is a story. *On the one hand, there is what it is possible to write, and on the other what it is no longer possible to write,* Roland Barthes said. My father's final story is no longer possible to write. It cannot be sentimentalized. It cannot keep its emotive qualities. It cannot be told as a story.

When it comes to my father's death, I fear the violence of my emotions. If the mind were a nuclear reactor with a built-in safety shutdown mechanism, I could say my mind shuts down when thoughts of my father's decline and fall occur. All the meters instantly go down. All the arrows suddenly point to zero. A peculiar quiet grips the rooms where only the blue fluorescent lights linger.

You are left with a story that is not a story. A novel that is not a novel, a poem no longer a poem.

When the plane descended over Portland, the sky was clear. Rafts floated down the Willamette River. A million automobiles went busily around on the highway cloverleaf. The sun was shining. After disembarking, I found my suitcase. It was going around and around on the conveyor belt.

I found a taxi and told the driver to take me to the Good Samaritan Hospital. He drove out along narrow little-traveled side roads. *All the streets into town are blocked*, the driver said. *We have to take a detour.*

I was thinking: it is easy to travel. It is easy to earn money with which to travel. This increased mobility has changed the meaning of the word *goodbye*. In former times, when people moved away, they did not see each other again. They shed tears of farewell. Now we know we will meet again. There are no farewells. A million airplanes fly in the sky on any given day.

When Canadian Airlines was promoting its program for the arts, they issued a poster. On it was a large and colorful picture under the heading *The Art of Flying*. Ballet shoes, typewriters, paint brushes could be seen flying in through the window out of the clear blue sky.

I was never afraid of saying goodbye.

My parents had a garden in a small town in the Willamette Valley. There they had apple trees, pear trees, cherry trees, blackberry bushes, azaleas, magnolia trees, dogwood trees, tulips, rose bushes, begonias, a hundred other flowers and bushes. They had a birdbath, picnic tables with chairs, a brick patio. Towering Ponderosa pines and Douglas firs stood overhead.

My father was always in this garden. He had a small red typewriter which he placed on the picnic table. Next to the typewriter was a large plate onto which he put crumbs. On the other side lay a stack of papers on which he was writing.

It would be a scientific paper in another language, full of calculations involving letters and numbers and mathematical signs in between. Behind his chair stood the trunk of an ancient cedar, half dead and hollow inside.

He had three constant companions on his authorial journeys through his imagined land of mathematics, geophysical explorations worked out on paper, and garden shrubs and flowers. One was a blue jay that hopped from the branch to the table to the typewriter to the plate with crumbs where it stopped its screeching, munched, then hopped onto the back of his chair. All this hopping was accompanied by loud screeching. The other was a grey squirrel with a large bushy tail that ran headlong up the cedar trunk, then down again, inverted, then onto the table where it stole crumbs from the plate, then up the trunk again. A third companion was a Siamese cat that sat peacefully next to his chair with an air of propriety, unmoved by the two divergent members of other species that shared its domain.

I often think this is the century of the countdown. We count down to the blast of the cannon and the opening of the chute on the aircraft that lets the bomb fall on some designated target. A city. A factory. A military base. We count down to the takeoff of the spaceship or rocket. We count down to the hour of Midnight on the Doomsday Clock.

Perhaps we should paginate our books this way. Begin with the last page and count down to the end.

It is good to remember that, before Christ, they were also counting down. Only they did not know it. They did not know what year it was. They could not say: this is 938 B.C. Next year will be 937.

We do not know what happens at Zero. If anything happens. Perhaps it is nothing. A sudden silence will grip the world. Perhaps there will be something: like an explosion in the sky. Bodies of seven astronauts will be scattered like dust over the fields of the high prairies. The farmer will turn them over in his soil, unwittingly.

I bought a mug to drink coffee from. Soon I had a huge house with many rooms, lots of light, and one ceramic mug. It was a relief to have nothing, but I suspected it would not last. In my suspicions, chairs, tables, desks, dishes, kettles, forks would begin to float in through the windows one by one. Out of the clear blue sky. It was just a matter of time, I thought.

The Gateway to the West has one long, wide, meandering boulevard which looks like a cross between Beverly Hills of the north and an English Mansion Row. This is called Wellington Crescent. On Sundays and holidays its residents are privileged to have their street closed to all traffic. Those who come in a car find a closed gate blocking access by vehicle. They have to get out and walk down the boulevard like everyone else.

I walk on the sidewalk until I get to the roadblock. From there I walk down the middle of the street. Joggers and runners go by in both directions. Men with babies, old women, middle-aged bachelors are walking both ways in the street. They are happy. Motorists, however, are forced to make a detour.

I was walking down Wellington Crescent on a day it was closed to motorists. An elderly man carrying two Safeway plastic bags, one in each hand, stopped as I passed him. He said to me: *I said to my brother Joe I said don't buy anything cheap it won't last.*

I got out of the taxi in front of the Good Samaritan Hospital, took my suitcase to the receptionist's desk, and asked where my father was located. She told me he had just arrived, Room 362. I left my baggage with her and went up to his room. There I found him in a bed, a forlorn look on his face, and my mother busying herself with cups of water and kleenexes. When I stepped into the room, he looked at me. No change of expression appeared, as if he thought I had been there all along. His knowing eyes seemed to say: here we are again, caught in a hopeless situation and this time we won't get out of it. What he did say was: *Hello again, good to have you back.*

*I never really left*, I told him.

Three solid days of tests followed. X-rays, magnetic resonance tests, blood samples, cat scans. Morning and afternoon the transport department came in their blue coats with stretchers to take my father to yet another exam room. The doctors promised that at the end of the third day they would appear with an accurate diagnosis and prognosis. Then we could choose among alternative courses of action.

I asked my father how the tests were after waiting. He endured them all in silent patience. He said they put his head in a machine and told him to keep still. *Of course when they say you can't move, your face begins to itch.*

It occurred to me: there will be an effort made to forget. There are things we will want to forget. Memory will become selective.

As my father grew more silent, until all there was were his lustrous light blue eyes, I knew he was thinking about forgetting. I told myself: I will not forget. There will be a book and it will be about forgetting. A book that refuses to forget even as it forgets.

*It is precisely because I forget that I read*, Roland Barthes said.

Grieving is remembering. Remembering intensifies your sense of loss. When people tell you: you will get over your grief, they are saying you will forget. That forgetting is condoned.

So I was thinking. I do not want my grief to go away. My father exists in my memory of him: not a selective memory but a whole remembrance. I want to entrap my grief in a place it will never escape from: here in these words. To remember forever.

Soon after my arrival in the Gateway to the West, it became very hot. It rained heavily for two days, with thunder and lightning in the clouds. Then as suddenly the sun came out and beamed down on the city with a vengeance, producing a mugginess unusual for the high prairies. Instantly five billion mosquitoes poured out of the swamps and attacked every warm-blooded creature within range. City council met in emergency sessions. We cannot get the better of them, they said. In the battle between man and mosquito, the mosquito wins. *They were here before we arrived and they will be here after we go*, a city councilor claimed to the press.

In the heat of the ensuing days, people began to wilt. Limbs were slumped over furniture. Activity slowed to a crawling pace. The concierge, on her way to the vegetable patch, got as far as the lawn chair and dropped into it tiredly. The cat, on its way to the second floor, got as far as the landing halfway up and collapsed in the corner. The song of the birds turned

into drawn out sighs. Even the mosquitoes lumbered heavily through the air,
too tired to bite. A dog sat on the porch
and wailed pitifully.

There is no winter in this text. I search for
signs of winter but in vain. There is no
memory of winter.

At the end of the third day the doctors
came, as promised, with all the results.
On every floor was a pleasant seating
area, with comfortable sofas and lounge
chairs and coffee tables. The paintings
on the walls and plush rugs on the floor
were designed to make the environment
pleasing. The two neurosurgeons led my
mother and me to the lounge area of our
floor where we sat down. They delivered
the prognosis without decorations: my
father had a nearly inoperable brain
tumor that had grown to a point where he
was incapacitated and only half his brain
was currently functioning. He also had a
resurgence of a former cancer of the liver,
which could not be operated on again.
Between his two ailments they reckoned

he had one to three months left to live.
They could try operating on the brain
tumor, but chances were one out of four
that he would die on the operating table.
Chances were three out of four that he
would suffer permanent damage from the
operation. They could give him chemo-
therapy for the liver, but chances were
two out of four that it would not work. If
it did work, it would only hold the cancer
in abeyance for up to a year, at which
point he would die anyway. If the operation on the tumor was successful, it would
grow back anyway and within a year he
would be back to where he was now. They
said they would get the operating room
ready and we should let them know in the
morning what we intended to do. Then
they left.

This is the part of my father's story I want
to bury under a thousand trivial words so
it will not be noticed. So I myself will read
them and forget what I am reading even
as I read.

My mother felt sick and glued to her lounge chair. She said: *would you go in and tell him this, I don't think I can?*

I left her sitting alone in the big chair after a long moment of silence. I had never seen her so small. I walked in the hospital corridors, passing room after room, my feet heavy as lead. In my nerves I sensed there was some purpose to this walking down hospital halls, but in my mind I was already forgetting what the purpose was.

Of all the things in your life that can go down to zero, the most comical is the bank account. I often think banks exist for the sole purpose of avoiding zero.

At the time I took the little red car and drove to the Gateway to the West with nothing but a red dress and a typewriter in the trunk, I had discovered that my bank balance was at zero. All the time I had spent with my father, I made no deposits. The bank immediately put the numbers back onto my balance sheet and made the transaction good by placing minus signs behind them. This way I could owe them money instead of them owing me.

---

What you do – brain surgery or chemo-therapy or nothing, with all the accompanying percentages – becomes a matter of numbers. I pondered how much time could be bought at what cost. How much quality time at how much suffering. I had the sinking feeling that it was becoming necessary for me to think for us all.

I took the elevator down, walked past the receptionist's desk, out the door onto the paved court in front of the hospital. Behind the building on a parallel street was a long avenue of boutiques, restaurants, gift shops, folk shops, bakeries, bookstores. Colorful ice cream vendors rang bells in the sun. Coffee stands were set up on the sidewalks; people in bright cotton clothes were drinking coffee from styrofoam cups, sitting on benches, on doorsteps, leaning against lamp posts.

I bought a cup of coffee, sat down on a bench in the sun and felt the warmth penetrating my skin. I had a ball-point pen in my pocket and a piece of paper. On the paper I wrote numbers. The numbers went as high as twelve and came in percentages of a hundred. Soon I had a graph.

One year earlier I was visiting my parents in their old farmhouse in the village of the Willamette Valley. The morning sun began to shine on the grass, reflecting flashes of light in the gossamer webs tiny spiders had laid over the green blades during the night. As I came down the stairs, I heard my mother call out in delight. My father was at the window. My mother stood behind him, holding clean cups she was about to lay on the breakfast table. When I came to the window I saw five deer, three of them young, only half grown. The youngsters were jumping several meters into the air, crashing around the huge yard. The adults were gingerly nibbling on the pink roses my mother had so painstakingly put down, eating them up. My father was smiling with a far away look in his eyes.

I did not know why we were not following a path. Perhaps there was no path, although I had seen a road on the south side of the small mountain. The pale brown dirt road curved as if it would go all the way around the butte in spiral fashion. Instead of taking the road, we were climbing straight up on the western side. The mountain was an infamous dry, hot, and waterless peak called Black Butte in the Oregon desert.

It was when I was still very young. I was hiking with a friend, a Danish American writer who loved the Cascades. It is a low mountain range covered with forest. Occasionally a towering peak rises out of the mass of lower mountains and stands magnificent and snowcapped in its pink isolation. *These are like the great spirits that rise out of humanity*, Erling said. Once in a while. Mount St. Helens. Mount Jefferson. Three Sisters.

Black Butte was so dry that trees could not grow. There were remnants of old forests, and some new forest to spite the conditions, but many of those trees crumbled in early death into the brown dust. Climbing up the mountainside, we had to step over the dead tree trunks that crumbled under our boots. You have to be careful of rattlesnakes here, he warned. *They lie inconspicuously in hiding, usually inside the hollow trunks of dead trees.*

By July sixth, war was declared on the mosquitoes in the Gateway to the West. People were no longer able to stand still because of itching arms and legs. Children showed up in hospital emergency wards with eyes swollen shut. The threat of encephalitis hovered like a cloud over the deceptively beautiful sunshine. The Mayor declared on the radio: *let's attack the damn buggers with everything we've got. Let's kill them all!*

I have noticed that the mind, like the body, compensates. It is said that when the body experiences sudden extreme pain, the brain instantly produces a substance much like morphine and shoots it through the system. The body does not feel the pain it feels until later. At night, when the lights are off and the house is quiet, the child realizes that the broken arm inside the cast is searingly painful. In the afternoon it had not hurt: when he came in from falling off his bike, his arm dangling in two pieces, it was only a mental shock.

If an impression is too painful, the mind shuts down in the same way. I often think: that is how soldiers can go on with warfare. Yet the impressions have not been erased. Later, much later, when all is quiet, they venture out of their hiding places. Slowly, cautiously, like rattle-snakes testing the conditions, creeping out of the hollow trunks of the past. If you step too close, they strike.

It sometimes pains me to know that nothing can ever be forgotten. No matter how much we desire to forget, it seems to me that *once an impression has been imprinted on the brain, it is there for good.*

It is good to walk about with no destination in mind. In the heat of the day I walked, looking at this prairie city. A native Indian boy, perhaps three or four years old, sat in the dirt outside the open basement window of a brick apartment building. His feet were stretched straight out in front and his hands were folded in his lap. His back was lightly bent over. He looked up with a sad face at passersby.

I went into my father's hospital room after pondering the situation in the corridors for a while. He lay on his back, looking at the ceiling. He knew we had spoken with the doctors. I could sense a mild anticipation, but his resignation was already so complete that whatever news I had appeared only a matter of curiosity. I sat down on a chair beside his bed. I told him.

Four years earlier I did the same: my father wanted the news from me after surgery for liver cancer. He woke up in the intensive care unit, hooked up to numerous machines and with an oxygen mask over his nose and mouth. Unable to speak, drugged nearly out of consciousness, he still had the force of will that characterized him all his life. I stood at his bed and he signaled that he knew it was me. He made some other sign with his hands. No one present could understand what his fingers were trying to say, but I recognized that with his right hand he was imagining writing on the palm of his left hand. I said: he wants a pen and paper. There was a rush for these items and we gave them to him. From the bottom of his morphine exhaustion, he scribbled almost illegibly: what did Dr. Moseley say? I bent over him and said clearly, to make sure he could hear every word: *Dr. Moseley said the surgery was successful and all your problems have been removed.* Then he was quiet inside his mask.

---

I have often thought: our ability to endure suffering is directly proportional to the amount of hope we have for something better.

As I suspected, items began to float into the second floor window of the mansion I had acquired as my own for a while in the Gateway city. A kettle, fashioned in Holland out of black steel. A white plate, a black saucer, a white cup. A pad to sleep on, two pillows. Two deep blue towels. A garden chair and table, white, began to stand in the sunroom. Here I put my typewriter.

I sometimes think it is not possible to keep an empty life. Life itself is material. It was a comfort of a kind to know that all the items around me were things I had never seen before.

It seemed to happen so suddenly: I discovered I was a stranger in my own life. I do not know when or how it happened, whether it was gradual or not, but I did not recognize anything around me as being of any *significance*. I began to wonder why people were going about their business so *importantly*. It all seemed to me inexplicably absurd. Somewhere along the way there had been a transformation

and I came back a different person. Someone no one recognized. Expectations went
unanswered.

I could see conflict coming in on the
clouds. Like the approach of a thunder-
storm. On the prairies you see it from far
away: a thick mass of dark purple cloud
that reaches to the ground. Streaks of
lightning flash out of it in various directions. You watch it move forward. Dark
bands stretch over the grasslands: the
rain.

That is when I drove away. To let the rain
fall down without me.

My father lapsed into total silence on
hearing the news I had for him from the
doctors and all their tests. I told him they
had given us twenty-four hours to decide
whether he would have surgery or not.

It was his way: when he had a problem
to ponder, he remained silent until the
answer presented itself. Like some Viking
chieftain who locks himself up to medi-
tate and will not come out until he knows
what to do.

I waited with him all night and all next day. He did not speak, but lay staring at the ceiling, then down at his hands on top of the blanket, then out at the window. Day turned to dusk and the lights of the city came on. It was the last room on the corridor, removed from the nurses' station and traffic. The night was quiet. Light from the hall fell aslant into the darkened room. My mother anxiously but patiently rummaged about the room with small paper cups of water, toothbrush, facecloth, whatever she could think of doing for him.

While we waited for him to commune with his own spirit, we did our own thinking. Each in our private way assessed the situation. I now think that everything we have been through since, and every emotion we have encountered, can be boiled down to those twenty-four hours. It occurred to me that to make a decision is to create a reality. An alternate reality. A design of fate that can never be rolled back to the beginning again.

*The Oregonian* carried an account of a man bitten by a rattlesnake. He was hiking in the Oregon desert. At the bottom of a ravine, he encountered a rattler and was bitten. Panic-stricken, he started to climb out of the ravine furiously. He climbed and ran until, a short time later, he collapsed and died. *His mistake was to run*, the article said.

*What you do when bitten by a rattler*, Erling told me, *is: sit down.* Stop all motion. The more you run about, the faster the poison spreads through your body and the sooner you die. *If you sit still, chances are you will survive.* Just apply basic first aid.

I conceived of an idea for a book: a man is bitten by a snake. He sits down and waits for help. The book consists of all his thoughts as he waits, the cloud of death hovering over.

When I was fourteen, I was to take the year-end examination in mathematics. It was a national exam, given to all fourteen year olds in the country. I had neglected to study over the winter, too busy with other interests: hair spray and high heels. My reasoning was: my father is a mathematician. He can show me in no time how to do these equations. When it comes to numbers, he can work miracles.

For breakfast we had toast and tea. I pushed my plate aside on the red table and put my math book in its place. I said to my father sitting next to me: *pabbi, can you show me how to do this?* He said: you mean you don't know any of it? I shook my head furtively, hoping my mother would not notice. We had half an hour. I pulled at his sleeve pleadingly. He looked at me in astonishment. After showing me the first two problems, he looked at the clock and said: *it simply cannot be done.*

I failed the exam. They must have given me a round zero.

My mother took to my graph, outlined in the Portland sun on that miserable afternoon, with interest and relief. Here was the situation clearly outlined on paper; the numbers were plain to see. It was a kind of cost-benefit analysis of the pros and cons of medical treatment and of no treatment. She showed it to my father and tried to think out loud with him, pointing at the numbers representing months and percentages. He was only halfheartedly following her, persistent in his silence. By the second evening he was not ready to speak yet. I told him we would decide in the morning and he nodded slowly. I informed the doctors they would know in the morning.

We were staying in a small apartment building across the street from the hospital, called Good Samaritan House. It was owned by the hospital and rented out for brief periods to family of patients from out of town. If they had gone out of their way to depress the distraught family members of the ill, they could not have done better. It was an old and worn down building. Paint was discoloring; rugs and upholstery barely held together. There was not enough ventilation through the building, so the stale air of hospital visitors accumulated and remained.

We had a suite on the second floor. To go in and out of that building, we had to brace ourselves. But it was a bed and a kitchen where we could make morning coffee. One night there was excessive commotion downstairs. We heard people running, doors slamming, a siren outside. In the morning, on my way out, I saw that suite number one was cleared out and all the furniture was out in the hall. I asked the security guard what had happened. *There seems to have been a murder in there last night*, he said matter of factly, chewing gum.

We were wandering through the deep woods of the lower coastal range of Oregon. The rain forest is thick with ferns and ivies and studded with pine trees. It was dark and musty under the cover of the foliage that shielded us from the sun. I did not know where we were exactly, but I was with a friend for whom these forests were home. We emerged from the dank foliage onto an open pasture unexpectedly. There the sun shone golden and inviting on the green grass.

We had only gone a few paces onto this jeweled play of various shades of green, beckoning like a mirage, when we heard gunshots. I could feel a bullet whiz by in the air. My friend grabbed my arm and yelled: lie down! We immediately fell on our stomachs, faces in the grass. Overhead I heard the shots zoom by, some just above our bodies. *It's the deer hunters*, my friend whispered. *They must think we're a couple of deer.*

There is no screen on the windows in the sunroom. When the afternoon sun shines warmly onto the aspen and elm trees, I lean out of the huge window. The breeze blows through the leaves on the branches and the trees shudder with a kind of unearthly delight. There are light green leaves, dark green, orange, brown, yellow leaves wafting up and down and sideways. I often think that green is the most soothing of all colors, the most comforting.

The color that makes you happy to do nothing except lean out of a window and breathe in the warm dry air.

---

During the night I stayed up and watched the lights go on and off in windows in other buildings. Noises from the street below floated in: cars passing, bicyclists on whispering tires; a laugh, a call, a heated conversation, a few words looming distinct, the rest barely audible. Perhaps I was not thinking so much as absorbing the time, the place. Rain came down in a few heavy drops towards morning. I could hear them splatter on the street like tiny water-filled balloons.

The small hospital room contained an orange vinyl-clad lounge chair that one could lean back and doze off in. The room was dark except for a night-light at the base of the bed. I could see my father's face in the dim light. He lay staring at the ceiling mostly and sometimes with eyes closed. At six a.m. we were to let each other know our thoughts. There was an invisible cloud of anxious anticipation in the night silence, broken only occasionally by an intruding nurse checking the i.v.

Towards morning I went across the street to our flat. My father was asleep. The air was moist from the night rain. The silver hue of daylight was in the horizon behind the roofs of rickety buildings. A conviction had been growing inside me during the night hours: I knew what we should do in my heart and it was nothing any graph could alter. A conviction like faith: it enters you in the form of a revelation and changes you. Its workings cannot be explained.

In the flat my mother was stirring from an uneasy sleep. As soon as I walked in, she called. I told her things were fine, put water on the boil, and freshened up. It was a bitter cup of coffee. Six a.m.

I sat in the front row of the university auditorium along with all the dignitaries and honorary recipients. The President of the country, the Minister for Education, the Minister for Culture, four men who were being awarded honorary doctorates, one of whom I was standing in for. Their families.

Before the convocations began, my father's name was called: Dr. Bödvarsson cannot be here due to ill health, but we would like to call on his daughter to come and receive his honorary degree for him.

I went around to the stairs and up to the stage. Suddenly the stage seemed enormous and walking to the podium in the center took an eternity. I was to stand facing the podium while my father's accomplishments were listed and his work praised. As I stood there, it felt like the heavy rain clouds over Iceland had descended onto my shoulders and were weighing me down. Finally the Dean of Sciences turned to me and stretched out his hand. I stepped forward, shook it, and took the enormous hard-bound folder containing my father's degree in the other hand. I walked over to where the President of the university stood in his blue cloak,

with white trimming down to his shoes,
and shook his hand. Then the tremen-
dously long walk to the other end of the
stage, down the stairs, and back to my
seat along the entire first row, passing
personages one could hardly ignore, yet
passing them without acknowledgement.
Knowing my father could not have taken
this walk: he would have stumbled, perhaps fallen. Thousands of people would
see him fall. The people of whom he was
proud and who were proud of him: he
would find himself humiliated.

When I came back to the hospital room,
my father was awake. It was time. I sat
down next to his bed and said: what is
your answer? He looked straight forward,
at nothing, and said matter of factly: *my
answer is what it always has been and you
know what it is.* As if it were self-evident.
As obvious as that you will fail your math
exam if you do not study the material.
I waited for him to finish. He had a deter-
mined expression on his face even while
he focussed on nothing in particular.

*I want no more surgery*, he said emphatically. Then he turned and looked me straight in the face. In his eyes were mirrored his four years of suffering, the sorrow, the exhaustion. The deep sorrow of it all.

In my mind a hundred dams broke and water flowed furiously out of the cracked reservoirs. I understood. I felt only relief that I did not have to argue my own convictions against anyone else's. I took his hand and he held his steady look into my eyes. I said with all my pent up emotions at bursting point: *pabbi, let's get out of here.* The i.v. bottle hanging overhead, the chart on his door, the clockwork medication, the anesthetist waiting outside the door to do his preliminary report. My father smiled. *Let's go home to the garden and the squirrel and blue jay and Siamese cat and the deer, the azaleas, the dogwood tree.* We tried to hold the tears back. But some of them broke through anyway. We were proud. We had a decision. We were in perfect agreement.

My mother walked into the room, tired from lack of sleep. Anxious. When she sat down, we told her. She sat frozen still for a few seconds and then breathed a huge sigh of relief. She said: it was what I also thought we should do. She embraced my father, kissed him all over his face, wept, said: can't we come out of this horrible room. We helped him into his wheelchair and rolled him out to the lounge area in the hallway where the comfortable sofas were. There we sat down and hatched out our plan of action.

My father announced his intention to pack up and leave that morning. Soon the various doctors were coming up to see him and telephoning in. You surprise us, Dr. Bödvarsson, they said. They grouped around his bed: the two neurologists, the internal specialist, the cancer specialist, the nurse. My father said to them, like a professor gently lecturing his students: *You may not understand that I come from a culture where to die in bed is the worst calamity that can befall a man.*

*Moments of happiness one forgets,* Mikhail Lermontov wrote, *but sorrow never.*

In the Gateway city I had one pot, made in Holland. It soon became clear to me that I no longer remembered how to cook. I had no idea what to put in the pot and how long to heat it. Even though I have cooked meals for many years, the knowledge had somehow left me.

I looked for a cookbook in the bookstore to show me what to do. There is no cookbook in the world called *Cooking for One* so I bought a book called *Cooking for Two.* It is always possible, I thought, that another person will come floating in along with other things. It happens.

As the summer advanced, the heat on the prairies grew more intense. It became necessary to sleep naked, on the floor, all windows open to the mild breeze that wafted in from the night. A welcoming breath of cool air, like a gentle soul blowing on the skin.

I lay in the dark room, empty except for
a foam rubber mattress and a navy blue
sheet. The room was large, the ceiling
high, and the white walls bare except for
an unused fireplace. The large old windows were open. Light from the lamp post
at the gate that marked the entrance to
my street reflected on the wall. Occasionally I heard someone walking below. A dog
barking. A car turning the corner. And in
between, silence.

I had no thoughts, only a sense of relief
that at that moment there was no one and
nothing to attend to. That it was pleasant
to lie in the dark and allow myself an
empty mind.

Soon I noticed a strange odor. It grew
stronger: a smell of chemicals, as if I
were trying to breathe the Winnipeg Inter-
national Airport. A yellow light began to
flash through the room, sliding from wall
to wall around in circles. I awoke out of
my half slumber and jumped up. It was as
I thought: they were spraying. An enormous truck was crawling along the

streets, with a yellow light circling on its roof to warn residents, and a spray of insecticides gushing out of pipes on its side, covering the trees along the street.

When mosquitoes fly into sprayed territory, they fall down dead. Others scramble away and die elsewhere, under leaves or between blades of grass. Every summer Gateway people raise the issue in City Council: how do we know for sure, they ask, that this chemical will not also kill us? There is a long debate until everyone is overcome by insect bites and a tacit agreement to spray is reached.

I closed the windows in all the rooms. It occurred to me that if I had followed the spraying report, I could have closed them earlier.

In the morning a red-breasted robin settled on a huckleberry branch just outside the screen. The sun was shining. He spread his wings and waited. All was still except for the leaves jittering on trees and the tin cones forever turning on rooftops.

Soon there were faint echoes of music in the distance: bells, trumpets, drums, high women's voices. In summer the Gateway city becomes a city of festivals: the Fringe Festival, the Street Festival, the Reggae Festival. In the park, the Folk Festival. In the zoo, Pandas. I imagine it is an announcement: there are passions out there. People still have fun, jump, shout. People with dreadlocks, in red tennis shoes, in white t-shirts with pictures of jugglers. Pamphlets lie scattered on corners that say: *just when you thought it was safe to go back to the streets . . .* and pictures of one man strangling another.

At noon, when the sky was light blue and clear, I thought: it is wonderful to be alone. To go from room to room in a slightly frayed mansion and think of a book. *A Hero of Our Time.* To come down a street on an overused sidewalk and think of grasshoppers. Unobstructed thoughts that meet no resistance.

But even then I was not quite alone. A cat resided in the stairway. Whenever I came

up the oak staircase, the cat was on the
bench under the stained glass window,
waiting. When I leaned out the window in
the sunroom, the cat was on the roof next
door, looking back at me. When I went
down to the cool basement to wash something, the cat was on the high windowsill,
leaning back relaxed.

So we drove back from Portland to the
little town in the Willamette Valley: my
mother at the wheel, my father in the passenger seat, and me in the backseat, arms
around his shoulders. He made the trip
in silence. It was a stretch of I5 he knew
he would never see again. The forests
of firs on both sides, pastureland newly
sown, Luckiamute River, Illahee Xing.
Exit 255, 254, 253, going down as you
go south. Roadside billboards that read:
*here today, lawn tomorrow.* And a fairy
tale amusement park in the woods called
*Enchanted Forest.*

*L'homme, c'est style*, say the French.
My father had a certain style. A certain

natural aristocracy. It was important:
to be above petty politics. To be above all
cynicism, bitterness. To part with your
friends *on your feet*. To make sure you
have a chance *to say goodbye*. In America
it is called: *dying with dignity*.

Because of the heat and dryness, the
forests of northern Manitoba began to
burn. The Pas, Norway House, Pikwatonei,
Nelson House, Pukatawagan, Snow Lake
were enveloped in flames. Eighteen thousand refugees fled to the Gateway city in
Canadian Air Force planes. The flames
jumped over the river *like it's not even
there*, a fire fighter shouted. Smoke filled
the northern regions. Soon rescue flights
had to be abandoned because visibility
was down to zero.

In the Gateway city, night streets remained quiet and calm, and stars could
still be seen behind thin veils of cloud.
But if the wind blew in from the north, the
air turned to smoke and breathing became
painful. Headlines in *The Free Press* read:
*the whole north is virtually blowing up
on us*.

The name of the town, translated from the Latin, was *Heart of the Valley*. The Willamette Valley is very wide and flat between Coastal and Cascade mountain ranges. Farmland, pastures, small hills, small towns. In summer a still haze fills the air and it is not possible to see the mountains surrounding the valley on the horizons. In winter it fills with rain.

My father was in the habit of hiking up MacDonald Forest. A minor mountain, thick with forest growth, and a gravel road winding to the peak where there was a good view of the valley. Along the road-side, ferns and ivies crowded. Pine trees, fir trees crowded for space in the woods. Whenever he saw a Ponderosa pine, he pulled a handful of needles off one of the branches and held them to his nose, breathing in the sweet perfume they exuded. I followed behind, enchanted by the luscious and strange forest.

It was almost midnight. I stood in line to rent a car in the Portland Airport. Business took me away from my father's

bedside for a few days. Between him
and Portland stood a two-hour drive. A
woman ahead of me got the last available
car and took me along as a passenger.
She was a graduate student in Forestry,
in the valley to do research.

I told her we often hiked in the MacDonald
Forest. She said: that's an experimental
forest. The strangest things go on there.
I asked her to name an example. For example, she said, *they blow the tops off the
trees* so the soil below will be nutrified by
the falling debris. They plant little bombs
at the tips and *blast the tops right off.*
Tree debris goes flying in all directions.

The old farmhouse in the *Heart of the
Valley* was two storied: downstairs, a
living room, family room, dining room,
and kitchen. Upstairs, bedrooms. Since
my father could not walk, we put a hospital bed into the family room downstairs
where he stayed. On one wall, shelves
were lined with his science books. On the
other wall, shelves were lined with straw

baskets of all sizes and shapes. The windows were made of glass prisms leaded together. There was an easy chair, a rocking chair, a television never used. A bright red cabinet of wine glasses with a collection of fifty jade elephants, trunks high in the air, stampeding off the edge: forever perched in furious stillness.

And the one indispensable object: a telephone. From his bed, raised at the back so he could sit up, my father dialed the numbers of all his friends, associates, and relatives around the world. *I have to tell them the news*, he said. To bid them farewell.

My mother and I nursed my father twenty-four hours a day in this last world of his. We brought him his food, helped him wash up, kept him company. We took turns sleeping on the sofa in the living room at night so we could hear when he called. We read to him from books and papers, dialed phone numbers for him, brought him his mail, measured out his medication.

Whenever I walked past his room where the door was always open, I saw him lying there, watching and waiting. His face was always sad, calm, and tinged with a sense of furious desperation. The house was quiet. Hours went by soundlessly. Finally my father said: *I cannot lie here with any greatness of spirit.*

We helped him into his wheelchair and wheeled him out onto the patio in the backyard. The spring sun was shining. Azaleas were in stark bloom. Tulips flowered. He put his red cap on his head and sat in his old place, head leaning slightly to one side. The Siamese cat sat down beside him. The old blue jay hopped and screeched about on the patio furniture. The grey squirrel reappeared and cautiously, nervously, approached the wheelchair with the attendant cat.

Suddenly the entire Canadian prairie cooled down. The sky was overcast. A hint of rain was in the air. People waited for drops to fall that never did. The temperature went down by ten degrees

Celsius. In the north, fire fighters began to have the upper hand. Thirty-six thousand refugees in the Gateway city became hopeful that they could soon go home.

It was at the time of the Street Festival. In Osborne Village, at the Portage Promenade, in Old Market Square, musicians, jugglers, dancers, comedians performed for passersby. They came in groups with street names: dancers who called themselves *The Flaming Idiots*, a magician named *Steve Trash*, jugglers who titled their act *Flying Debris*.

In the cool evening I heard the faint sounds of violin and guitar. People clustered around yellow tents, listening. A bicyclist in black with a bowler hat cycled across the lawn carrying a violin in a black case. A woman from Southeast Asia crossed the street with a bundle wrapped in green cloth on her head. A propeller plane ground through the air above.

I am glad there are such times in life: when you are protected by your solitude. When whoever speaks to you must speak

to you on your own terms. Times when
you do not give an inch. Because all you
had to give has already been given.

It occurred to me: even love runs out
when who you love has taken it away
from you and is unable to bring it back.
Then you have no more.

Except for a treasured space, perhaps,
where what is left is something you guard
with your life. It is your rope when you
scale the cliffs.

I am told my father climbed mountains in
Nicaragua, with pick axes and ropes. I did
not see him. I am told he climbed in the
Montana Rockies and fell in an avalanche.
He was assumed dead until he stood up
and walked to the road. I did not see this.
I am told he careened down an icy path in
an automobile in the Coastal Range of
Oregon and miraculously came to a halt
without damage. I saw nothing. And an
airplane he flew in Central America almost
crashed. Of that story he said: when we

were about to crash, I thought *at least I am not perishing in my bed.*

I rounded the corner in the little red car. It was early evening, when the light is deep and colors are stark. The water in the Red River was deep blue, navy. A pleasure boat sailed slowly up the stream and under the bridge. At the edge of the bridge a policeman stopped me. He said: *you can't go across, there's a Folklorama parade and all the streets to downtown are blocked.*

*Cats* was in the Gateway city from New York. On the stage, cats were sitting, lying down, standing, leaning on precipices, sitting on oil cans, jumping over boxes, floating up on rubber tires. They sang a lot and danced a great deal. As they did, Great West Life ran an ad with a picture of ballet shoes, violin, paint brush, oils, spotlight. Underneath it said: *The arts. The staging of civilization.*

I have seen the blank page referred to as a stage. All that happens on the page is theater. Writing is a play. Words are actors, props, singers, dancers.

I think of civilization as a great contrivance. A great book.

It occurs to me this is about the ability to start a new life. When you are at Mile Zero. Before you go up in a spotlight.

My father's surgeon knocked on the front door of the house. He was an elderly man of medium height, grey hair, gentle smile. He came into my father's room, sat down beside his bed, asked him how he was doing, assured him it was the right thing, rubbed his back. He said: *I am here as a friend, not as a physician.*

I think it is possible to be many people at once, so long as you announce which person you are before you step in the doorway. Before Dr. Leman came to visit as a friend, my parents were distressed. My father lay in his bed, his face tight with tension, his eyes staring, distraught with guilt, regret, sorrow, uncertainty, longing for the ordeal to end. My mother jumped up at every small sound, unable to sit still, rattling dishes in the kitchen, washing towels a hundred times, driving herself in the possibility that *something else could have been*. When Dr. Leman left, they were both calm, serene, tranquil. *You are doing the right thing*, Dr. Leman said. My father was grateful: I saw it in his look. He was so grateful he could not speak. Even the tears that rushed and gathered behind his eyes were unable to break through.

I thought: someone who can give comfort like that to the dying is not a physician, not even a friend. He was here as an angel. It was an announcement he did not know he could make.

The American people, I began to realize, are preparing themselves to be angels. More and more people will be dying in their homes like this. Of incurable terminal illnesses: AIDS, cancer. And we must all learn to give, I thought.

Two hospice nurses visited. They sat down with my mother and me and discussed what we could expect. They spoke with my father. They said they would come to help whenever needed. Home health nurses came with stethoscopes and blood pressure gauges, inflatable bathing basins, thermometers. One of them, Claudia, sat down with us in the living room. She said: is there anything you would like to talk about? You must talk about your feelings. *If you don't talk about how you feel, it will come out in other, worse, ways.*

Because I did not take Claudia's advice, when it was all over and my father's story was complete, the world as I knew it fell apart. I found my life in shambles in the dry prairie: papers were strewn all over the floor of my study, my desk, in boxes, in corners. Letters, phone calls, messages remained unanswered. Deadlines passed by. All my nerves seemed to have been clipped and I broke down at the slightest criticism. Wet clothes hung over chair-

backs in the living room, dining room,
hallway; in the sink dishes were piled, on
the counter food leftovers, on the floor
crumbs, strips of lettuce, bits of bread.
On the deck rotting leaves, in the flower-
beds weeds five feet high. In the basement
a rock and roll band, five teenagers shaking the walls with amplifiers turned up
high, electric guitars, drums, cymbals.
There was shouting from one floor to
another, telephones ringing at five minute
intervals.

I was shaking, I wept and was unable to
handle what was supposed to be the real
world. The man I lived with said: don't
feel sorry for yourself, *get on with things.*
So I begged: *can't we have some quiet?*
*I want the world to stop!* When there was
no response, I saw that the world had only
stopped for me and not for anyone else.
It was only *my* father who went to the
grave. He was no one else's father.

That was when I took the little red car and
drove to the Gateway to the West and the
odometer went berserk.

*Neither reason nor sense nor greed nor pity nor perspicacity nor worldly wisdom nor expediency nor filial duty gave my hand into yours. No one can say I was carried away in that hour,* Elizabeth Smart wrote.

She is talking about love. And she is talking about writing: *in spite of everything so strong in dissuasion, so rampant in disapproval, I saw then that there was nothing else anywhere but this one thing.*

That writing is *a poverty-stricken word against the highly-financed world, yet it is not meagre, it is enough. I do not accept it sadly or ruefully or wistfully or in despair. I accept it without tomorrows and without any lilies of promise. It is the enough, the now, and though it comes without anything, it gives me everything.*

I think there is nothing owing to you when you come into the world. And only those you have loved will mourn you when you go.

There was a knocking on the door. It was downstairs at the back door to the concierge's floor. A pounding that would not let up. No one answered. From my sunroom above, through the screens on the open windows, I heard the knocking. It was a cold morning, overcast and windy. Overnight rain had left the streets and grasses wet. It was Sunday and the Gateway city was slowly opening Folk-lorama Festival pavilions. I opened the only screenless window and looked down. On the steps to the concierge's back door stood a young woman with pitch black hair. Behind her was a large black German Shepherd dog who looked up at me. We stared at each other.

My mother and I took turns sleeping in the living room where we could attend to my father during the night. One would stay up till ten, the other would do so from ten until six in the morning. Each of us, for this reason, slept only every other night.

It was a large living room and the cot stood next to my mother's large loom containing a wallhanging in the making: wool woven in beautiful gold and brown patterns, but abandoned. A small touch-lamp was lit in the farthest corner so it would not be completely dark. Beside the cot was a small table with a clock radio lighting up the hour and minutes in bright red letters that went from twelve: zero to twelve: zero. I put my head on the pillow, trying to rest. In the other room I heard my father's uneasy breathing. Then my name and I rose. It would be for a drink. Or a wash. Or company. And at midnight, I counted out nine different kinds of pills in various amounts.

Soon both of us were exhausted from lack of sleep. We were dragging our feet through the days, unable to brighten up. The clouds in our heads grew thicker and darker until the purple hue showed through around our eyes. Finally we hired a woman to stay between ten and six. Her name was Ramona, a Californian of Mexican extraction, slender, small, with pitch black curly hair. My father called her *the lady from Catalonia.*

Every day my father's friends came to call. They came one at a time and sat by his bed. On good days my father sat in a wheelchair in the living room and visited. His colleagues, friends, former students all came to say goodbye. When a visitor entered and asked: how are you Gunnar? my father said in his heavy accent: *I am sorry you see me here in this miserable condition.*

My father was a senior Professor of Oceanography at the university in the valley, and later Professor Emeritus. His special field was geophysics, and within that, geothermal heat. He was trained at first in engineering, then geology, mathematics and physics, and he received his doctorate from the California Institute of Technology under the Nobel prize-winner Richard Feinman.

But it was what he brought from his Nordic culture that set him apart in the academic world. He had many doctoral students under his supervision. He saw them all through: no one who came to him went away without a degree. He never abandoned a student. If they had difficulty, he worked with them until the problem was solved. If office time proved less than enough, they came to his home. He befriended them, opened his home to them, had them over with their families at Christmas, lent them his cottage on the coast. He stood by them and they were grateful.

When we drove into town from the Good Samaritan Hospital in Portland, my father returning to his final hours at home, we rounded the corner of our street. There, in front of our house, stood a cluster of students waiting. They had come to help him into the house. They were silent. They were sad. During his illness, they had come to read to him from academic journals, newspapers, books, for his eyesight was by then too poor. They had helped him into a wheelchair, rolled him into the yard, and sat with him in the sun: no more inclined to abandon him than he them.

In his last days they telephoned from all over the world as the news of his condition spread: from China, Arizona, Texas, Sweden, Iceland, Lebanon. One former student from the Middle East, settled in the U.S., phoned in desperation. Fouad said to my mother in a broken voice: *please take care of him, he is the best friend I ever had.*

It is because we all admired him. We all took our cues from him: *this is how to be a human being.*

Twice a day I went for a walk. It was good to get fresh air and in April the air in the valley is perfumed with blossoming magnolias, cherry trees, honeysuckle. It was dazzling to see on every side such profusions of flowers, and blossoms hanging overhead from branches dropping their silken petals onto the sidewalk and grass.

Nature was filled with gifts: and that was a mirror of the people in the town. I did not know there was so much love in the world. Every day, neighbors appeared with meals and fruit and bread so my mother and I would not need to spend time cooking. Mary brought lasagna, spaghetti, salads; Joanne brought stews, soups; Jinny brought barbecued ribs; the Smiths brought coffee cakes; Susan left fresh baked breads on our doorstep; Dr. Leman brought fresh strawberries; a barbecued chicken appeared from neighbors we did not know down the street. There were many more: we were overwhelmed with gifts. Flowers came from all directions until the whole house was charmed with the bright colors of blossoming chrysanthemums, azaleas, Persian violets, roses. Even Judy, the cleaning woman, brought flowers every time she came to clean house: flowers which cost her half of her morning's wages.

It occurred to me that I had spent a long time in the scorching prairie where the dust blows up in whorls and the wind

eddies on street corners, where the dry
air is pierced in spring and autumn by the
hoarse calls of geese migrating in forma-
tion over the plains. Where the severity
of summer, the high altitudes that chisel
deep lines into parched faces, hardens
the soul. I had forgotten what a luscious,
mild, damp, gentle climate does to wake
up the sleeping soul and give rise to
human affection and generosity. I had
forgotten how such openness takes away
all fear and makes you able to trust again.

Every time I saw a house for sale in the
little town in the valley, I had an inclina-
tion to phone the realtor and buy it. I
thought as I took my daily walk in the still
morning, after a sleepless night on the
cot and in the kitchen and by the sickbed:
*I want to start a different life. To forget
about all that has passed up to this day.
I want to move here and live here forever
as if nothing else existed.*

In spite of festivals, on long weekends the
Gateway city becomes deserted. Sidewalks
are empty of pedestrians. Very few cars
drive up the street. Restaurants are open

without customers, waiters loitering
empty-handed in doorways. Half of the
inhabitants in the city have cottages on
the lakes in the north. A quarter of the
other half go to northwest Ontario or
British Columbia or the Rocky Mountains
for holidays. Only the sick, injured, and
pregnant remain. People either too old or
too weak to travel. Those who are healthy
and still in the city end up feeling: *there is
something wrong with me if I am still here.*
They look over their shoulders, worried
they will be recognized. They are reluc-
tant to answer their phones. They hide
in dark movie theaters showing sleek
American films in nearly empty cinemas.

On such empty days the small squirrel
I sometimes saw among the branches
of the elm trees in front of the house
paraded freely along the telephone wire.
Whenever I looked out the living room
window, the squirrel was either walking
on the wire between poles or lying down
midway, tail and head hanging down over
the wire.

A butterfly with black and yellow wings frequented the flower patch at the side of the mansion where I lived. Whenever I stepped out and walked down the driveway, it flew across my path.

I thought: these are the signs of familiarity. The small notices that we are sharing space in nature, that our homes overlap. When you move into a house, it is not just a house. It is an environment: other species lived there before you and will after you go.

Around the house I lived in was a pretty garden. The front lawn was broken in the middle with a large flower patch and on the sides were other flower beds, all crowded with yellow, orange, pink blooms. Rosebushes girdled the house and huge pots of bright red geraniums stood on both sides of the steps.

It was midnight. The streets were quiet, birds were asleep, lights were off in all windows. In the sunroom the single lightbulb glared unnaturally against the stark black night outside the screens. Electric light seemed just then a rude invasion into nature's gentle show of moonlight and shadow. I heard a whacking and rustling in the leaves outside. Looking out I saw the concierge's teenage grandson on a rampage with a butcher knife: chopping down the flowers in the beds and the leaves from the large green plants that dignified the mansion. Little brown and yellow and pink and red flower heads rolled and lay haplessly on the grass.

We were in the Rocky Mountains where we had gone to hike along one of the many trails. We wanted to take a steep path that would show us a view of the peaks and valleys at the end. We drove to the beginning of the trail as described on our map, parked, and set off.

The path was wide at first, but as it ascended it became narrower until there was almost no trace of a trail in the thick undergrowth. Soon we were deep in the bush of the mountainside forest without a sign of a hiking trail anywhere. Charles said: this is no hiking path. *We've gone up a goat trail.*

The first thing Ramona, the night lady, said to me when I met her was: *take care of your mother, I see it happen all the time. The wife exhausts herself taking care of her sick husband and becomes the first to go down.*

The sand was warm. I buried my toes in the grey grains of sand at the edge of the water. Lake Winnipeg was unusually calm: the surface was unperturbed by wind. Only very faint ripples wiggled onto the beach. Wind surfers failed at staying afloat. Sailboats further out stood still. Swimmers dived under water and re-emerged elsewhere. On this beach there are no shells or seaweeds or starfish. Only sand and small stones.

I sat in the warm haze through which the sun did not quite emerge. The soft summer colors of the prairie had a soothing effect: pale milky-grey water on the lake, light grey and beige sand, soft green leaves on aspens and birches, pale yellow wheat fields stretching across the plain.

I was thinking about a letter I had received from a friend in Denmark. Hans wrote about my father's passing: *the only consolation I can give you is that you will never get over it.*

---

In the summer most small towns in the prairie have their own festival. Gimli has an Icelandic Festival. There is a fair; amusement rides are erected in the park; boat races set off from the harbor; foolhardy visitors set themselves up to be dunked in barrels of water. In the park wares are sold: books, sweaters, ceramics. By the pavilion is a large stage, and seats are arranged for hundreds in front. On Monday of the long weekend, speeches are made and music is played and poems are read from that stage.

That summer the Festival was graced by an official delegation from Iceland: the President of the country, the Minister of Culture, the Mayor of Reykjavík, the Ambassador in Washington. Along with them were the Premier of Manitoba, the Minister of Culture for Canada, the Mayor of Winnipeg. The ceremonial stage was crowded.

I took my friend Joan to Gimli. We sat on chairs in the sun and listened to the speeches. The people on the podium were all very familiar to me: *it was so good to be a tourist.*

It was a good friend who presented the toast to Iceland: David Arnason, the writer, stood up in his black suit and imposing grey beard. During the course of his speech, he said: Iceland has produced world class artists and achievements out of all proportion to its small size. This is because they know that talent is everywhere. *If a country wishes to survive with its culture and integrity intact, it must nurture the creative talents of its own citizens. It must protect its own culture.*

All of a sudden many hundred pairs of hands were clapping madly against the sun-laden blue sky.

It was my father's birthday. When I tried to sleep the sound of the crowd was in my ears and scenes from my father's last moments haunted my mind.

It was in the early days of his confinement, when he often was in his wheelchair in the living room or out on the patio in the back. I helped my father into the chair and rolled him to the fireplace. He asked me to put on the record he had always kept for special occasions: Hans Hotter singing Schubert Lieder in his deep sonorous voice. I did so. Every time he heard this, my father struggled with tears. He sat in the wheeled contraption, head leaning over to one side, and wept from the depths of his sorrow.

When I was small I often went with my father on his geological expeditions around Iceland. We sometimes went to Krísuvik in the south: there was a very small lake in the jutting jagged lava. The water was absolutely turquoise and green, with the smell of sulphur in the air. It was a gem to see: water of such a beautiful hue that I was spellbound. My father told me: *this lake has no bottom, it goes on down forever.*

I had nightmares of falling in: of falling down and sinking in the water forever.

A nursing student from the community nursing school appeared at our door. She asked to be allowed to help sit with my father so my mother and I could rest. Chris said: *please let me help, it is important to me.* Three hospice nurses were always there when needed. Ramona's daughter was waiting to be allowed to help with the nursing. The physiotherapist made extra visits to chat with my father. Marilyn said: *I want to remember to do the things that are meaningful.* Home Health nurses came and bathed my father, washed his hair, kept a chart of his vital statistics. Every day, women were there, assisting. Volunteers. *It was an army of women.*

It occurred to me to wonder what had marked these women out from the crowd. Why did they come out to help people in need? And soon I detected from words dropped into a sentence or occasional comments that they themselves had suffered some form of loss in the family or illness or crisis. That they reacted to their own suffering by reaching out to others. And somehow, it was a good thing to know.

*Literature itself*, Roland Barthes wrote, *is never anything but a single text: the one text is not an (inductive) access to a Model, but an entrance into a network with a thousand entrances.*

I allowed myself to imagine that deep within our souls there is something we all share. That each of us is simply an entrance into that common arena.

It was David Arnason's cottage, near Gimli, close to the water of the huge lake. *The world's thirteenth largest freshwater lake*, the plaque in Gimli said. The water was grey and silty, the sky overcast. Small waves threw themselves on the thin strip of sand where green stalks and yellow straws grew out of the ground. Outside, on all the walls of the cottage, covering all the screens on windows and doors, were hordes of dead flies. So many corpses of flies were plastered against the cottage that it was barely possible to make out the color of the wood underneath.

My father's condition deteriorated rapidly. Soon he was no longer able to get into the wheelchair. Confined to his bed, eventually he could not turn himself. For every move, he needed assistance. For every sip of water, every change in position, every time his forehead needed drying, our help was required. We became his eyes, arms, legs. His extension to the world. The more we took on his being, the deeper that ton of lead inside me sank.

There was something my sister did not understand about this. She was not in the same world somehow. I tried to say to her: *everything is different. The world has ended: the world we knew.* But to her, things were basically the same as always, only a bit worse.

I could not talk to her: suddenly there was an insurmountable gap between us. I did not want it there but was powerless. I was in her flat stacked with mathematical papers, pictures of sailing ships, astronomical charts. She sat back in her chair, unmoved.

Perhaps I was exhausted. Perhaps the self I knew had already departed from me. I left her place, got in the car to drive back to my parents' house. It was night. Awaiting me at the house was the withering body of my father, the strength of our family. And the fading mind that once charted the scientific world with light and activity. The one person who I knew cared unconditionally, receding into the abyss of timelessness. Driving through the empty night streets of this American small town, I suddenly found myself screaming at the top of my lungs.

I knew then, that night, that I had reached rock bottom. Somewhere in the great depths of the soul that is reputed to go on forever, there is a floor. Ground zero. Where you have gone so far down that the only movement possible is up again. And I knew I would not move from this place for a long time.

I sat with my father and could not keep the tears from falling. He was alarmed when he saw us cry. It was the one thing he did not want to see. He stared at me intensely. It was our sorrow he feared, not his own. Perhaps it was then he decided it was time to go. His eyes were slate blue, like the great Pacific Ocean in the early morning before the sun rises to make it glow.

Soon the big German Shepherd dog I saw on the back steps of the mansion in the Gateway city took up residence in the backyard. Every time I looked out, the dog was rolling himself over on the grass and scores of flies were busying themselves over the dog food dish.

The cat that had previously been ruler of the roost found itself displaced. Whenever I came out on the stairs, the cat ran crying to me, plastering itself against my feet.

The summer quieted down into early fall. The intense heat went away and instead comfortable temperatures and sunshine blessed the Gateway residents every day. The crab apple tree outside my sunroom windows grew pale yellow. The apples became larger and pink in color. Berries were suddenly noticeable inside dark green foliage: tiny bright red points of focus.

On the streets long-haired roller skaters with backpacks dashed in between pedestrians. Pregnant women sat lazily on benches waiting for a bus. Beggars became fearless: *you wouldn't have enough for a cup of coffee, thank you ma'am.*

In that far West I dream of, the Pacific coast, there is a tiny harbor village. Depoe Bay, *the world's smallest harbor*, says the sign in front of The Spouting Horn.

I took my son on a boat, *The Kingfisher. This is the place where they filmed One Flew Over the Cuckoo's Nest*, I informed him. We were taken a few miles out where no land will appear for weeks. The motor of the boat was stopped and we sat on the water billowing on the undulating ocean. Suddenly a massive grey form rose out of the sea next to the boat: a being so crusty and laden with barnacles that we might have mistaken it for land had it not moved and spouted a stream of water high into the air as it rolled serpent-like before us. *Sometimes they stop and allow us to pat the top of their heads*, the skipper said.

A week after we had returned home, we learned that another such boat had mysteriously capsized in the same place. The passengers were immobilized by cold when they entered the freezing water and perished.

The novelty of being alone in the Gateway city soon faded. Things that were special at first became ordinary: listening to the wind in the leaves in the early morning. Watching the squirrel roll itself over in circles in the elm branches. Seeing bees fly in through the huge open window, take a measure of the sunroom, and then fly out again. Feeling the quiet hours pass as the sun changes position, without pressure, without intensity, without tears.

The concierge, Jo, was gone. Perhaps to Mexico to find a place to live: the woman who never wanted to see another Manitoba winter. The mansion had a new owner I had never met. A lady from Germany. I could see that my days in that warehouse city, the prism of the West, were drawing to a close.

Many poverty-stricken native people lived outside the gates of my street. I would see them in groups of twos and threes every time I stepped out for a walk: holding large Coke bottles, carrying children, walking without unity or pattern, some-one always lagging behind.

In front of me were three Cree natives: a man, a woman, and a teenage boy. The boy was bare-chested, holding a navy blue t-shirt in his right hand. He walked behind the other two. A small white butterfly fluttered across their path and into the bushes under the hospital wall. The boy jumped after the butterfly into the shrubs and began whacking it with his shirt.

My mother's sister flew in from Copenhagen to be with my parents at the end. She was a soft-spoken woman of fifty, with such a mild manner and gentle demeanor about her that her presence did much to soften the blow of what was happening. In the mornings Birte came down with a bright smile, had her coffee and cigarette in the garden, and then went to work washing and cleaning with constant good cheer.

It occurred to me how wonderful it is to be able to admire one's own family.

It became harder and harder for my father to take his medication. He was sometimes unable to swallow the larger pills. His will to take them began to give.

*What is the point of taking these pills?*
he asked with impeccable logic.

His appetite went away. He slept more and more.

My mother went in to wake him up for lunch. It was noon and time for food and pills. She shook him for a while, but he remained asleep. After trying for about ten minutes, she came upstairs to where I was. I can't wake him up, she said, alarmed. I went down and tried to shake him, talk to him, call him. There was no response. We stood for a while, uncertain what to do.

By his bed he had a little hand bell to ring if he needed us and we were out of the room. I took the bell and rang it in front of his face. He opened his eyes instantly. Eventually he was eating and things were normal. I asked him: *did you hear us when we were trying to wake you up? Yes*, he said. *What were you thinking?* I asked. *I was thinking,* he answered, *now they are going to give me those miserable pills again.*

It occurred to me that people who are comatose *can still follow everything going on around them*. That their *presence* in the room should not be underestimated.

The Dean of Sciences at the University of Iceland said to the crowd: when Dr. Gunnar Bödvarsson was preparing to go to North America, he came to my office. In his hand he carried a book which he handed to me saying: *I would like you to keep this for me while I am away.* I told him I would take good care of it. Then I saw it was Edward Gibbon's *The Decline and Fall of the Roman Empire.* It has since occurred to me that he left the book with me *so I might read it.*

It was called *Shólahús – The Schoolhouse.* A small but stately building bequeathed to the University of Iceland. It stood on one of the old streets of Reykjavík, over-looking the town pond. After the cere-monies at the University auditorium, a smaller group walked to the *Shólahús* for a reception to honor the four recipients of honorary doctorates. There were hors d'oeuvres and glasses of wine. It was Presidential election day. Among the guests were the President of the University, the Minister of Education, the President of Iceland, the Dean of Sciences, the Dean of Social Sciences.

Soon the other three honorary doctorates had all given a speech to the selected assembly, thanking them for the occasion and adding something thoughtful. It occurred to me that since I was standing in for my father, who was too ill to be there in person, I ought to speak for him. I stood up to do so.

The light was low and I knew it would not get dark. It was June. Swans swam on the pond below the house, and across the street were the walls of the cemetery where my grandparents were both buried. *It did not even cross my mind that my father would never make it back to join them.*

Since, I have often said to myself: *be careful where you live for you may die there.*

The light that poured into the Gateway city in the morning and evening was deep and rich. The sky was absolutely blue and clear, so pale blue that the eye is transfigured and hallucinates forms in the utter emptiness that produces such a color. Blackbirds flew across the bare panorama with confident wing strokes. A small grey airplane showed its underbelly with a drone. Every day seemed to compete in beauty with the day before. The grey squirrel began to free-fall from branch to branch: starting at the top it dropped itself down onto successive branches where it wagged as the branch gave way to the weight.

Yet I thought: it is beautiful, but I am not healed yet. Something is still in me that has not gone away. If I go among people I feel threatened: that whenever someone opens his mouth to speak it will be to say something abusive to me. That my emotions will be held up to ridicule. I will be criticized.

The hospice people left a sheet of paper with us when they visited my father one day. The sheet said: *Symptoms of Grief. Do not be alarmed if the following conditions occur, it is normal when a person experiences grief*: excessive fatigue; inability to cope with noise; severe change in sexual habits; depression; development of the symptoms of the deceased; lethargy; *fear of people*; a desire to hide; excessive weight on symbolism; a need for ritual; bouts of weeping; hot flashes; inability to cope with everyday details. *Do not try to hurry the process. Understand what is happening.*

My father's friends and colleagues, some from the distant past, even childhood school days, were visiting at first. They drove up from California, flew over from Washington, D.C., drove in from the coast. But eventually he was unable to receive them. When Arvid came to chat and sit on the folding chair by the bed, my father fell asleep in mid-sentence. When Don and Jo White came to spend some time in the living room with him, he leaned over in his wheelchair and dropped off to the side in uncontrollable sleep. When Jónas Haralz was there to spend a few days, my father could not keep the train of thought going and lost contact repeatedly with the topic. Friends all went away in sad silence, knowing they were saying goodbye for the last time.

It was one of my father's geological expeditions in the southern Icelandic countryside during my childhood. I walked away from the small group of scientists who were doing a form of surveying I did not understand. Nearby was a small mountain composed almost entirely of barren rock face. I climbed the steep cliffs, ascending higher into the pure blue air of an Icelandic summer. The rock face was whitewashed and the view as I climbed higher was more and more expansive: tundra I did not particularly like. Lava lay round about in old crusted formations, black and jagged. Moss grew over the openings in the hardened rock, disguising traps small people easily fell into.

When I got to the top of the mountain,
I was accosted by an Arctic tern. It flew
over me close, then away a good distance
where it turned around and sailed back at
me with incredible speed, like an Air Force
bomber on a desperate mission. Wings
spread wide, it lowered itself over my
head and attacked the top of my head
with its beak. I knew I had come too close
to a nest. There were other terns preparing to do the same. Only too late did I
remember my father's warning: *if you go
up there take a frying pan with you and
hold it over your head.*

My son was seventeen years old. During
my father's confinement, school released
its students for a three-week break. He
took the plane from Minneapolis to
Portland, carrying his violin in its case.

It was morning. The valley was shrouded
in summer haze. The Albany pulp mill
issued foul-smelling clouds into the air
from its huge chimney. I counted the exits
as I drove to the Portland Airport to pick
him up: 258, 259, 260. Cushioned in the

pine forests I noticed brand new shopping malls and apartment complexes. At the airport I found him: dark jeans, abstract t-shirt, shoulder-length brown hair, violin.

For the next three weeks he gave his grandfather his daily shave with a dose of improvisational jazz thrown in. He became the grocery boy, buying all the groceries and carting them home in a van. He helped lift his grandfather in and out of a wheelchair. For the rest he was off exploring the valley and taping library records onto cassettes.

Often my father asked his grandson to play for him on the violin. It was a Romanian piece, newly learned for a school concert, that became the favorite. Every day there was a tiny concert. My father listened raptly. I thought: now perhaps I finally know *what all those violin lessons were for*.

The three weeks the boy was there, *somehow the picture was lit up with sunshine*.

The way an empty sky can become translucent with light, and though there is nothing there, it is beautiful.

After the boy left, my father no longer called on us. He no longer wanted to know what we were talking about in other rooms. When we came in to him, he looked at us, but his thoughts were far away. Instead of speaking, he held our hand.

The days in the Gateway city became monotonously warm. The only clouds in the sky were thin flimsy ones that stole in on the afternoon but were never substantial enough to block the sun. Air-conditioned charter buses drove slowly through town, a woman with a loudspeaker in front reciting city attractions to tourists: The Forks, Wellington Crescent, Osborne Village, The Zoo. Mosquitoes were still around but had stopped biting. Ticks were gone. Blackflies were bored with the same garbage every day which the garbage truck forgot to pick up.

Instead, dogs went mad. Formerly placid household pet dogs yanked their chains off their collars and followed children down the street for hours. When children stopped and showed fear, the dogs growled and started tearing at their clothes with wet thirsty teeth.

I had to go away for five days. We could not really tell how long my father would remain in his present condition. Meanwhile, all the parking meters in my own life had, so to speak, gone to zero. The yellow disk was down and the red one was up: the one that said *time expired*. So I left my father in the hands of my aunt and my mother with the assurance that if things got worse I would be on the first plane back.

I did a whirlwind rush through six cities: Portland, Minneapolis, Winnipeg, Regina, Calgary, Salt Lake City. Long enough to put new metaphorical quarters into my waiting meters.

Salt Lake City Airport was very hot and stuffy, crowded with people of all descriptions. Young girls dressed up in color-coordinated outfits with earrings and purses to match. Old fat women who barely fit into the plastic seats. Suntanned hikers striking up conversations across seating aisles, wearing khaki-colored shorts and Birkenstock sandals. And the Forestry student I was to catch a ride with into the valley from Portland: the one who told me about the oddities of MacDonald Forest.

While I was gone, my father's condition fell into a slump. There were conflicting reports and forecasts did not all agree. He was sleeping nearly all the time, they said on the phone, and no longer eating much. Then, as I turned to come back, he was better. Others said: *you always get a little better just before you go.* I was in a great hurry to get back. The slow-moving line in Salt Lake City was suddenly too exasperating.

When I entered the house I could see something had happened. There was a look of desperation on his face as if it had become hard to breathe: breathing had turned into the focus of all his energies. His eyes darted back and forth restlessly and he was not talking. We were not sure he could recognize everything. My mother said to him the night I arrived: *do you know who this is?* He said *yes* determinedly but with difficulty. Who is it? my mother asked again. My father answered, looking hard at me, as though it were self-evident: *this is Sjana.* But the look on his face seemed to say *pardon me a moment, I seem to be drowning.*

After that he never said anything but *yes.*

In late summer moving trucks appear with greater frequency on the streets of the Gateway city. Houses that have been up for sale all summer begin to show "sold" signs on the front lawns. Huge moving vans back onto driveways and block off the streets while men load up furniture. Well-kept lawns are suddenly neglected during the change of owners. Grass turns yellow, flowers droop, ferns die while still upright. Booths that sell lottery tickets are swamped with people checking their numbers: hoping their numbers will match enough to send them to Florida or Hawaii.

Restlessness sets in: the German Shepherd in my backyard no longer lay patiently on the steps between geranium pots. Instead he plodded angrily along the fence, around the yard, through the vegetable patch, stopping at the gate to bark and at the door to look in. The elm tree in the next yard came alive with squirrels. They no longer sat still in the branches. Instead they threw themselves from tree to tree in daring acrobatic feats.

I sat with my father all night. He had begun to breathe rapidly. He did not seem to be asleep, yet he was not awake. Sometimes when I asked him a question, he was able to whisper *yes*, sometimes not. Since he was not awake, he could not drink any water.

I wetted his lips with the hospital sponge we had been given by the hospice nurses. When the small sponge reached his lips, he bit at it with as much eagerness as he could muster.

In the morning he was still hyperventilating but no longer answering. I stayed by his bed. Thinking he could still hear me, I talked to him. I talked to him all morning. I thought: if I do not talk he will not know I am here. It will be less lonely for him that way.

It was a Saturday. A beautiful sunny morning none of us had paid any attention to yet. My aunt came into the room. I noticed the bristles on my father's cheeks. The sweat on his forehead. Some little voice in me said: *he wants a shave and a bath.* For the next hour Birte and I bathed him, shaved him, combed his hair, changed his shirt. I thought: he always wanted to arrive clean shaven wherever he went. He refused to meet guests without shaving first. He would want it this way.

When we were done, I stepped outside
into the backyard for the first time that
day. The blue jay was at the birdbath.
The azaleas were flowering in bright red
blooms along the edge of the garden.
I was tired and only vaguely absorbing
the lush spring that blossomed in defi-
ance of our mood.

As I stood there my sister opened the
door and yelled: *mother is calling for you.*

I ran into my father's room. My mother
was bending over the bed. I could see my
father's breathing had become erratic:
chaotic. He was gasping as if he were
awake, but he was not awake. The body
itself, as if without the will of the owner,
was struggling for air: for control. My
mother was desperate, at a loss.

I saw right away what was happening.
Birte and my sister came into the room,
running. Without fully knowing why,
I started to give orders: *Birte, grab my
mother. Gunna, phone Kathy the hospice
nurse.* And I took my father's head in

my arms. *Talk to him*, the little voice in me said, *talk to him*.

And I did: I told him it was all right, it was just a little difficult patch and then he would feel so much better. *In a little while you will feel much better, we just have to get through this.*

Then he was not breathing. The body, longing for breath, heaved for air one more time. Then once again. Then nothing.

My mother had her face in her hands. Slowly she came up to my father on the other side of the bed. I wanted to reassure her. I said: *it is finished.*

When I was nine years old, there were graduation ceremonies at The California Institute of Technology. My father was to receive his Doctorate and he had on a floor-length black gown with a cap and tassel. I did not know exactly what a Ph.D. was, but I knew it was something to be very proud of. The ceremonies were on the lawn, outside in the sun. I had a pale purple dress with a black velvet collar and black velvet buttons. It was a beautiful dress of which I also was very proud. And white gloves on my hands, a pony tail, and bangs. I was photographed holding my father's hand: he in his black gown, I in a purple dress. It was a beautiful spring day. All the flowers were blooming and the palm trees were swaying in the breeze. Perhaps it was the happiest day of my childhood: everyone was so happy that day.

Perhaps because they knew fall was coming, the animals around the mansion became furiously active. They would either have to dig holes for themselves where they could hibernate for the winter or else fly far away to the south for many months. Swallows crowded in the eaves troughs of the house against the garden. A red-breasted robin was settled in the huckleberry bush outside my window, feasting on the small red berries every day. All the elm trees round about were filled with dashing squirrels scurrying between branches and trees at record speed, their long tails flurrying behind them.

I began to look around me as well. My time to leave was coming: I would have to get into the little red car someday soon and drive to a new place. It was moving season. Developers trying to sell newly constructed condominiums placed billboards in front, reading: *if you lived here you would be home now.*

It was a Saturday morning, eleven thirty. I remembered later to look at the numbers. I often wondered about the importance we attach to numbers: how we imbue them with significance at critical times. In his illness my father repeatedly asked: *what time is it?* Even in a completely incapacitated state, as if he needed to go to a meeting or catch an important flight. His favorite poem was Goethe's *Doctor Faustus*. A tiny passage from that grand play had been photocopied many times and lay strewn around in his study for continual reference. The passage said:

*When the hand on the clock falls, then time is over for me.* Sometimes in the morning, when I came downstairs to find him awake in his bed, I asked him how he was and he would answer with a small crafty smile: *the hand has not fallen yet.* As if the passage of every hour he could count were a personal triumph. That this was a match of wits between him and the clock.

*There is no zero on the clock.* To get to zero, you have to step outside of time.

People came and took my father away. Before they removed him, we all went in to say our final goodbyes. I kissed his forehead and I knew he was no longer there. This body we were going to attach such importance to – bury it in the ground and cover it with flowers – was not him. He was gone. I knew for the first time that, despite my confidence all these years that it is easy to catch a flight and return to the people you pretended to say goodbye to before, it sometimes happens that a person goes away and will never return. *You know he will never return.*

They took the hospital bed and the wheel-chair away. We cleaned up and put the cot back where it was supposed to be, and the tables and chairs. As if this had been an unhappy play and we were stage hands demolishing the set. The principal actor had already gone home and we had to stay on a little while longer.

Even though it did not make me afraid, I did not have a good feeling: *when I looked around I discovered that all the clocks in the house had stopped.* None of them was working.

Above the town that is called *The Heart of the Valley* is a lilting green landscape where huge ancient oaks grow. Their crooked forms spread out in all directions unhindered, and their crowns hover over the pasture majestically. From there it is possible to see the Cascade Mountains in the east and below them the soft green acres of the valley and the clusters of dark green fir trees in between. It is a peaceful place where birds sing all

summer and the sunrise spreads its red
wings over the waiting land.

That is where my father is buried. He lies
under an oak tree: in the heat of the summer day, there is shelter under the heavy
branches. In the downpour rains of the
West, there is cover. On his granite head-
stone is carved an image of his beloved
mountains and a Ponderosa pine.

When I saw the beauty of that final resting
place, even though I was not inclined to
think there was anything good about the
story of my father's decline and fall,
I somehow felt grateful. Grateful that
there had been no pain in his final illness.
That it was such a gentle and soft depar-
ture, almost like the whispering rain at
the window that you hardly know is there.
If someone asked, you would not be able
to say with certainty that it was raining
outside.

Perhaps I had disappointed thoughts:
disappointed at being left behind. I always
wanted to go with my father on his expe-

ditions: into the heather where loud plovers stand on tufts, crying through the endless summer days of the Arctic. Onto the black sands where heavy ocean waves crawl in from the sea slowly, wearily. To scale the cliffs where seabirds have left their eggs to hatch in the naked sun. To dive under the ribs of the ocean, looking for sunken Turkish sailing ships laden with treasures.

*This time you cannot go.* That little voice. Perhaps I felt unhappy that I had to turn back and walk tiredly across the huge lawn where the departed lay under gigantic oak trees. I have to go back and busy myself with people and their million deadlines, dates, timetables, charts, machines that circle around zero, threaten, and never get there. Perhaps.

At five in the morning the streets of the Gates in Winnipeg are like a picture someone painted without people. Or a deserted movie set. A slight illumination of dawn has begun, adding an eerie luster to the darkness of the night. The large houses along the street are touched with a perception of life. All is silent.

I got up. Every time I stepped, the hardwood floors boomed out in the quiet of the night. I boiled water for tea in the black kettle and sat down by the front window. There was a wicker chair and a windowsill for my cup.

From there I could see out of the Gate and into the streets closer to downtown. Occasionally a car drove up to a door out there, someone got out and stumbled inside. One person fell down on the street. Another person came out and helped him in. I could only see the outline of their silhouettes. Then all was empty again.

Somewhat later I saw two figures slowly walking up the street. One was leading his bicycle. They stopped at the corner and talked for a while. Then one walked away up the side lane. The other, pushing his bicycle, continued towards the Gate.

I recognized my son's light, leisurely walk. I heard the familiar clap of his Birkenstock sandals. On his head was the favorite Peruvian hat a friend had given him. Under his arm was the inevitable violin. *He is the one*, I thought, *in whom all my father's hopes are bound.*

The boy turned up the driveway to the house, locked his bike, and came upstairs. I opened the door. He came in, took himself a mug of tea, and sat down cross-legged on the living room floor. He opened his violin case and put the violin on his shoulder.

The city was about to awaken. Soon the first rays of sun would burst in through the curtainless windows. The first notes of a new melody sounded from the violin. I knew soon all the empty rooms would fill with music.

Printed in Canada